PEACE, PEACE
THEY SAY

Martine van Bijlert

RAINFED PRESS

Epigraph: Jeremiah 6:14 and Ezekiel 13:10-11a (NIV).

Published by Rainfed Press
Cover design & art: Martine van Bijlert

Peace, peace they say/ Martine van Bijlert -- 1st ed.
ISBN 978-9-08345740-6

For the peace makers

*They dress the wound of my people
as though it were not serious. 'Peace, peace' they say
when there is no peace.*

— Jeremiah

*Because they lead my people astray saying 'Peace'
when there is no peace and because, when a flimsy wall is built
they cover it with whitewash, tell those who cover it with
whitewash that it is going to fall.*

— Ezekiel

Contents

PEACE, PEACE THEY SAY

Author's note

In 2022, I joined a month-long peace poetry postcard exchange. As I sat down to write about peace, I kept turning to war, wondering whether I would stand out – a sender of dark collages and words that refused to sound upbeat. A poet who kept reaching for memories of aftermath and foreboding.

I've spent a large part of my life surrounded by ripples of war. I used to have images to work with, a sense of a whole: Peace like a river. Swords to ploughshares. Everyone sitting under their own vine and their own fig tree in undisturbed places of rest. A higher power that could be made to act, a universe bending towards relief.

Somewhere along the way, I lost the words. So many of them had been drained and emptied of meaning, dumped in a sea of project speak and programme acronyms. Peace became a political ambition, a deliverable, an agreement between elites. A narrative that needed propping up, a trade-off to temper calls for justice. Behind the declared peace, already the contours of new conflicts in the making, old ones still smouldering. Everywhere already the beginning of an aftermath.

I knew better how to talk about peace, before I worked in peace building.

But I kept returning. For three years, I joined the peace postcard exchange, sending short bursts of thought to strangers while the world around us bucked and roiled. The first year was marked by the aftershocks of regime collapse in Afghanistan. The second year brought the death of a close friend. The third year, the relentless bombing of Gaza while governments looked away, mouthing *self-defence*. For three Februarys, I felt the dissonance of receiving poems about moments of beauty and calm – music, friendship, birdsong. Felt the dissonance of reaching for those images too.

This collection is a gathering of those poems, each a thought long and in conversation with the others. Written in the gap between *but still* and *but also*. Because how can we not write about beauty and calm, essentially hope, when battered by turmoil? But also, how can we?

So we live. We can't be overcome by despair and we can't pretend it's not there. We can't keep calling peace what isn't peace, but we also can't disparage what is, or what could be, however insignificant it might feel. We should speak of it, even if we can't find the words. Because we need to hear from people who no longer know what to say.

Martine van Bijlert

You will be signing up to exchange peace poetry postcards with 29 poets (fledgling or accomplished) and discover what you have to share about peace. It's a simple practice where you write and mail daily thoughts about peace as short poems on one fresh postcard a day, until all 29 people have been sent a card with a separate expression of peace.

This practice intersects with our human development at every level. Cards explore peace in all the ways, how it intersects with our planet's climate crisis, as counterpoint to the loss of community and optimism due to the Covid pandemic, current national and international affairs, and as a path to justice.

As we reach out to each other on the topic of peace, we are taking time to create peace, first as we imagine it, then as it shows up on the postcard. Many of you have shared how you have found the daily practice of writing and sending out a peace postcard healing and reassuring.

*— email introducing the 2024 World
Peace Poets Postcard Exchange*

February 2022

and on this first day

I realise I know
how to write
about

riddled bodies
a whole country
in mourning

how to listen to
longing and people
who still dream

how to feel anger how to
watch the young their
eyes still shining but

I don't know

where I left this
elusive thing

that was given to me
for safe keeping too

when a country is hit
by not one war but

two or three
even four

when peace is made up
of pockets of safety

reports of skirmishes
and remnants

that need to be
mopped up

the kind of peace

that needs a PR
strategy and

is a success
only when

your side's
in charge

in the silence
after the shooting stops

before people go about their days again

and politicians come rushing in
and aid organisations

and stories
need to be
told

about who won
and why

      in that silence

between inbreath
and release

that stillness

asked what they thought
peace would be like

they talked about
schools

going to see family
without fear maybe

some
sightseeing

not being on edge all
the time

not that noise all
the time

it didn't happen

it still didn't
happen

the longer you've

    worked for peace

        the harder it gets

            to know what to wish for

    power's not very good

    at being good
        for people

        it needs to happen
            between us I guess

how not to sound naive

I guess this
is going to be

a very
short poem

walking into an office

to find you staring
at a wall calendar

a picture of the Alps
in garish green
and slate blue

      imagine

you said

spending even just
a day there

your gaze almost
apologetic

come join my fleet

    we'll visit new planets

        wear uniforms
           in muted colours

                time will stretch
        and collapse

      make us patient

    no longer
an audience

we don't even know
    if anyone

        is still looking for us

  and by now
    none of us is
      sure

        we still want
          to go   back

isn't it interesting

how in Star Trek – even after years of

        wandering through space

the ship still looks pristine

with never any cleaners
anywhere

nobody overworked
or underemployed

        untethered

from any chain of command

everyone still turns up in uniform
tidied up and on time

when did it become so hard

        to talk about peace

not talking about the calm
of a slowly lapping lake

the stilling of a thought

but what we used
to believe in

no more going to war

no more speeches to cover
up indifference

no more pretending
a life is not a life

war doesn't stop for weekends

only   sometimes   for Christmas or Eid

sometimes   it wanes for no
reason anyone can see

        — like an inbreath

filled with quiet pleading:

                please, somebody

        can we have it too

this daily miracle of

being safe
in your own home

can we talk about peace building

about saying bodies
and meaning institutions

saying agreement
and meaning a document

pulled from the storms
of suspicion

it almost never holds
says my peace studies mind

oh the miracle of guns
no longer shooting

        says the rest of me

oh the silence of the skies

to my right the sky
grey and heavy

        to my left

a hazy blue with
undecided clouds

like someone who hasn't been told yet

like someone who
sails into a bad news room
with sun-flushed cheeks

but wait
behind the grey

        now light

peeling
away the flatness

even on a day
radiant like this

I imagine the sky

full of the ghosts of
frantic prayer

         shot through

    — even after all this time —

with blazing
flashes of relief

a drone a drone   25

flies as if to
the moon

unseen

a day a day
without this hum

this dusting
of uneasiness

while I was away

summer swept in suddenly
rained down sun and coaxed out buds

bursting with impatience

leaves unfolding everywhere
shiny and tiny

and abashed
by their own brightness

when you come out of a war

    seemingly unscathed like

           let's face it
              most people do

     (because
       there's always
         so much worse)

   it can make you
     feel like you shouldn't

       live too much
         or too loudly
           not too happily

  some people wail and some people go silent but

slowly I'm starting to believe that the ones like us
  who mute ourselves

          out of respect or shame or
       guilt over what we didn't
     ask for either—

I mean there's such a thing as a life force

  I mean look at the trees   pushing out their
  buds each year   the flowers   with their
  blazing colours   the birds testing the air after
  a storm tore at their branches

I can still feel the surprise

of suddenly being
a new being

the whole world
shimmering when

          touched

do we get second
chances like that

does it take falling in love or

simply falling between
the cracks of

the carrying beams
of our lives

does it take putting down
your crown

being the monarch
who walked out

          and —they still can't imagine it—

won't come back

the mountains

made me
giddy

I took pictures
without thinking

it felt   not unending

but close

        this you who loved
   so unguardedly

is still with me

men in robes

sauntered

down a hollowed road
lined with trees

backlit and in
no hurry

dust filled the air
like gold

like softness

February 2023

a fridge

     a fridge

is what people mourn

when their city's been
reduced to rubble

     sometimes

some things are
easier to grieve

than others

to travel your own country

visit your own
village

stay with
your parents

to no longer feel reckless
when you say what you think

while you're a little drunk
and so tired of how

narrow

the future
feels

how threadbare

stitch

is what you do

while you're
waiting

for something
to happen

something
to start

life can become a little complicated

when bringing
the powerful down

looks like it might
affect you too

      peace rarely means

things staying as
they were

it takes a while
to settle down

maybe if we slow down

we can become
like seeds

small explosions

with delayed
release

weird disturbances
that spark

fondness
        hope

I can't help but ask

is happiness always
built on oblivion

and forgetting

always stacked on
the bodies of the tired

silence

held taut

is the bed
from which

the river
rises

what was war called

before we had
countries

and laws on
who you could kill

and who not

as if war could
move through

        carefully

    like a cat on a crowded side board
       snaking between vase and picture frame

have you not seen
those velvety paws

     tapping a glass bowl

as if casually curious

what the crash would
sound like

a friend of mine died   43

        like we all will

     except this
was so early

and I don't know

what this has to do
with peace

except that
everything is tangled

always

has thinking about peace

       always been complicated

          has every generation
               grown up thinking

      it has to happen
        somewhere else

        (what is it
            I'm asking?

how do you work for peace

when your country
is at war when your

government is so
afraid it surveills

and detains when
the rules are

stacked against you
how do you

keep going

I wish I lived

in a world
where the word

    board

made me think of
board games

or cardboard
boxes

not board rooms
or boarding

school or water
boarding

I've been trained

      in the tradition of

            theory of change

        logframe
      inputs outcomes
    risks and assumptions

but what it
comes down to

must be love
and determination

being a person
in your time

as best you can

my friend died

and I'm not grieving

the books he'll
never write

        but the hole

burnt in the fabric of time

the rooms that will
never get to greet

his stooped
frame

Benedictine Abbey

where I watched the monks
sing their way through
six services a day

hands stacked under
the folded banner of
their cassocks

precise
unhurried
movements

still I have no
words for peace

last night I was awake

listening

to a lone bird sing
itself through the dark

I woke to rain

wanting to know
where I could

learn a song
like that

Benedictine Abbey

where monks
live their life

like the strokes
of a broom

no need to
enlarge or

invigorate

I wake and think

if the world slowed again
I'd be happy

tired of skimming

wanting to land

February 2024

some people think

bringing down power
is all it takes

others say: talks

however hard
till an agreement

makes for
fragile magic

      I say hope and
this soft air

and struggle and
talk and love

and love

you know what they say

    no justice no peace

    and how it's hard
    to find people strong

    and gentle enough
    and how the new

    is always infused
    with the old and

    how it's hard to
    know what

    to ask for and
    of whom

the messy work

of hoping
for a miracle

while wading

through

the mud of
trying

you've heard them say

      peace like a river

      but I remember

      mountains seen
      from up high

      that sudden ribbon of green
      that vein capillarying

      into side valleys

      fields orchards
      homes

someone sent a picture

to a group I'm a part of

that said: I did not come
to bring peace but to

bring the sword and
why would anyone

want to send
that anywhere

without adding
a question

peace

no longer
the complete disregard
of how you're trying to make a life

      your house
      no longer porous
      to anyone who wants to enter

            the day no longer a trapdoor
            to powerlessness

imagine a lake

a ripple

the round sound
of a drop or jump

silence
suddenly alive

what do you do then

in this world wracked

by death falling
from the sky

to keep writing
and wrestling

is what life is made of

peace grows not just
where there's
calm

I stood at the river's edge

    waiting for it to speak

      it was moving
         away from me

   foaming

     folding in on itself

  moving

    staying

I've done the trees

the lakes, the birdsong

the quiet that descends

at the heart of it

is this

                    a few moments

            days, preferably

      longer

in which you are
no longer
afraid

I lay in bed

     counting my breath
       backwards from

           eighty-eight
             to zero

     to see if that would
     still my thoughts

        thinking of all the you's
          across the world

     hoping for sleep
     a new day to wake into

         breathing in fear

      breathing out hope

    breathing in shelter

a woman walked in
wearing yellow

and I thought
I want to be

like that

bringing sun
into a room

without
even trying

writing about war

        is also writing about
peace you say

but I'd like to
    know how

      to imagine it
        into being

think about buying
a new coat walk

into a gallery feel
out of place assemble

the IKEA three step
ladder fill your

mind with song
while cooking

the kind of life
you wish you

could wrap
and send to

so many places

you say ocean

    I say pacific
        trash vortex

you say birdsong

    I say yes please

       but also

all those people

       deafened

by the sound of
    their house gone

one night

I stepped outside
faced the wind

pulling at branches

yes, I said

    I'll join

not knowing
what I signed up for

(other than life

so

what kind of
small prophet

are you

and what will your
wasteland be

what will you say and

which particle
of the wave

will you become

how long does it take to travel

from atom to atom

to cross the void

    what would you find

if you could
enter that

silence

some days

I find myself
saying to myself

          I need
                a new theory
                        of change

what I mean is

I need to gather
myself

return to the
string of

incremental
failures that

          hopefully

adds up
  to hope

waiting

for the wind
to return

the breath
that rushes

leaves along
the street

pulls a sheet
of sand across

the beach

goes this way
and that but

      where did it
come from

don't skimp

     on your prayers
     you said

        let them fly

     as if I'd dream of
     holding them back

     but who is listening
     is the question

     that undergirds all

    life
       art
          protest

you can't see
the wind

but watch the
branches move

grass leaning
under its touch

water hurrying
home

we don't know
how far

our words
will carry

stand at
the edge of
the river

see what you
can reach

Postscript

I've been asking myself for weeks where my anger
went / and why I can't aim it because / to be
political these days is to be angry / and clear like a
bell / truth to power they say but / what truth and
what power because / to be political these days is
to be smooth / and to be political is to be brazen /

is it true birds imitate the sound

of weekly protests if they go on long enough / is it
true our technology shapes how we present / and
thus perceive / and thus present ourselves / like
my sister years ago who started to sound like / the
soap operas I never watched / I've become
cautious imagining cutting comments in a faraway
world / where I rarely even speak and / the people
I agree with are / angry and say / why so silent we
see you / (the new order will be for the trodden)
because / this is power and it is small and delicious
/ and this is anger and it is righteous / and
delicious / and these are voices and those are
crowds / and you must join /

I agree with everyone who disagrees with me

my politics have become silence / I refuse to need
to join a crowd and / maybe I no longer have the
patience / to be one of the dogged ones / who
push and pour their lives into the / incremental
failure on which change is built / the slow work of
living a conviction / beyond the confines of my
house / to say this is the foolish rock I'll try to climb

I disagree with everyone who sounds like me

I tried and the forces were bigger and / change
brought its own problems / better always also
brought worse and / to be political these days is to
be battered / maybe it was easier before I'd
spoken / clear as a bell and futile as a gong / and I
can't see a movement I want to join (make your
own / even just a wave of one

    particle loose cannon miniscule and silent

steadily building / and the horrible truth is the
digging up of children / will not stop the war / the
showing of their little bodies / will not stop the
war / and now to speak of war has become the
crime I'm told and / in my funnel people are eyeing
each other saying / why so silent so complacent /
living as if not affected while the days / hang heavy
around our heads

Acknowledgements

Thank you to the editors of Otis Nebula and Oyster River Pages for publishing earlier versions of *come join my fleet* and *when you come out of a war*.

Thank you to many others: Wayne Milstead who never got to see this (I miss you) and Aaron Tighe, for your friendship and for being a home for so many writers; Roxanna Shapour for seeing the heart of this project; Sari Kouvo and other friends at Elin's Era for the ongoing conversation about conflict and change (which is really about peace); Holly Wren Spaulding, Moira Walsh and the Poetry Circle – Kortney Garrison, Fritz Eifrig and Heather Mackay Young – for companionship and feedback along the way; Carla Shafer and the participants of the World Peace Poetry Postcard Exchange; and of course Jorik, for a life together that works.

MARTINE VAN BIJLERT is a mixed media poet, artist and writer who grew up in Iran, now lives in the Netherlands and in between worked as an aid worker, researcher and diplomat, mostly in Afghanistan. Find their work at www.martinevanbijlert.com